HOCKEY THE NHL® WAY
Win with Defence

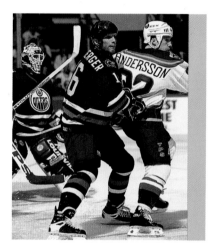 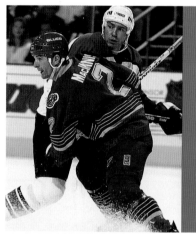 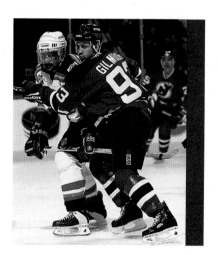

Sean Rossiter &
Paul Carson

GREYSTONE BOOKS
Douglas & McIntyre
Vancouver/Toronto

For Vladimir Konstantinov, master of the lost art of body checking, who led the National Hockey League in plus/minus with +60 in 1995–96.

Greystone Books
A division of Douglas & McIntyre Ltd.
1615 Venables Street
Vancouver, British Columbia
Canada V5L 2H1

Canadian Cataloguing in Publication Data
Rossiter, Sean, 1946 –
  Win with defense
  (Hockey the NHL way)
  ISBN 1-55054-644-9

  1. Hockey—Defense—Juvenile literature. I. Carson, Paul, 1955 – II. Title III. Series
GV847.25.R684 1988 j796.962'2 C98-910452-4

Editing by Anne Rose, Kerry Banks
Cover and text design by Peter Cocking
Instructional photographs: Stefan Schulhof/Schulhof Photography
Front cover photograph: *Paul Kariya & Viacheslav Fetisov* by Brian McCormick/
  Bruce Bennett Studios
Back cover photographs by Bruce Bennett Studios. Photographers: *Brian Leetch,
  Eric Lindros:* John Giamundo • *Mike Modano:* Layne Murdoch • *Kelly Buchberger,
  Doug Gilmour:* Brian Winkler • *Al MacInnis:* Jim McIsaac
Printed and bound in Canada by Friesens
Printed on acid-free paper ∞

Every reasonable care has been taken to trace the ownership of copyrighted visual material. Information that will enable the publishers to rectify any reference or credit is welcome.

The publisher gratefully acknowledges the assistance of the Canada Council and of the British Columbia Ministry of Tourism, Small Business and Culture. The publisher also acknowledges the financial support of the Government of Canada through the Book Publishing Industry Development Program for its publishing activities.

Contents

The NHL Way team

Our players

Nicolas Fung

Daniel Birch

Scott Tupper

Kendall Trout

Brian Melnyk

Kellin Carson

Jordan Sengara

Brandon Hart

Will Harvey

Tyler Dietrich

Rob Tokawa

Michelle Marsz

Jesse Birch

Special thanks

Special thanks, first and foremost, to the parents of the NHL Way All-Stars pictured on this page; also, to the NHL—Brian Burke, David McConnachie, Denise Gomez, Arthur Pincus and the players who have shared their secrets; to the staff of the UBC Thunderbird Winter Sports Centre, who made us feel welcome; and to Chris Brumwell and the Vancouver Canucks organization, for all your favours.

 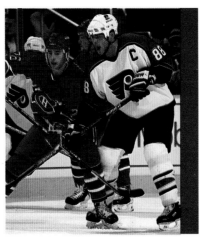 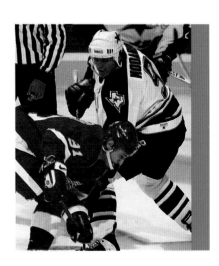

Our coaching advisory staff

Paul Carson
Coach coordinator, the British Columbia Amateur Hockey Association

An assistant coach of the UBC Thunderbirds, Paul Carson is also the provincial coach coordinator responsible for coach development programs in B.C. He is a master course conductor for the NCCP, and coached high school hockey in Sendai, Japan. He recently completed work on the Nike Hockey Skills series.

Terry Bangen
Special consultant to the NHL Dallas Stars

Assistant coach with the Vancouver Canucks (1996–97), Terry Bangen coached two national junior teams, including the 1996 world champions. He has coached three Kamloops Blazers Memorial Cup champions—with Ken Hitchcock, Don Hay and Tom Renney—and was head coach at McGill University in 1995-96.

Ken Melnyk
Author, the Hockey Skills Development Program, Tykes/Atoms

Named coach of the year (1995–96) by the B.C. Amateur Hockey Association, Ken Melnyk was on the organizing committee for the 1988 Winter Olympics. He wrote the Games' deficit-free business plan. However, Ken's most notable achievement may be Brian Melnyk, one of our NHL Way players.

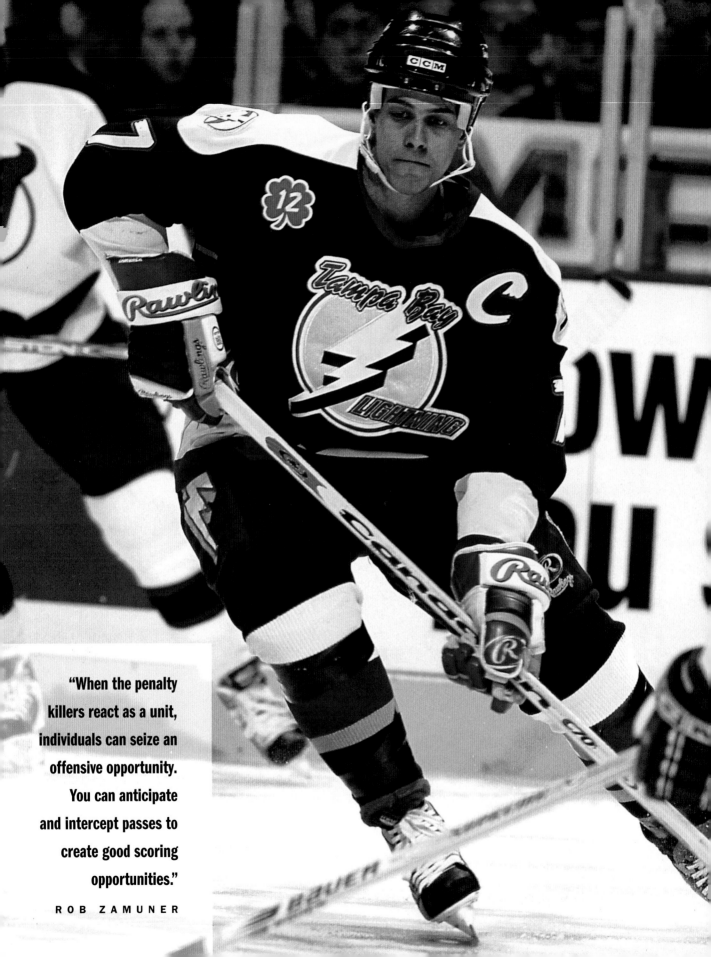

"When the penalty killers react as a unit, individuals can seize an offensive opportunity. You can anticipate and intercept passes to create good scoring opportunities."

ROB ZAMUNER

Foreword

The skills you need to be an effective defender—and every player on a hockey team is a defender at least half the time—are easily learned. But they require constant practise to perfect.

Defensive skills are not secrets, though you seldom hear about them from so-called hockey experts.

To begin with, to be a good checker you have to see the game better; your head has to be on a swivel. Good defensive play starts with being aware of the game around you, and responding to what you see. Coaches call this "read-and-react." You "read" what other players are doing, and you "react" to it.

For example, by watching how well the puck carrier is controlling the puck, you decide whether to attack the puck, or back off and contain your opponent. We tell you how.

You have to be able to skate in any direction: sideways and backward, cut sharply either way, stop, and start fast again. Montreal Canadiens assistant coach Dave King calls this "quick feet." No good defender ever stands still for long.

The single most important lesson any defender can learn is that you don't need to have the puck to dictate what will happen with it. Learn how to invite the puck carrier to do what you want. Soon the puck will be on *your* stick.

Knowing how to play without the puck will make you a more valuable player. It will keep you in the game when you're on the ice, but don't have the puck. Your teammates will respect you. And, best of all, your coach will put *you* on the ice when the game is on the line.

Ken Hitchcock
Head coach, Dallas Stars

Introduction

At least half of hockey is defense—more than half, when you think of how often the puck is up for grabs. Even the best players have the puck for less than a minute in any given game.

That leaves 59 minutes or more when players with average skills can make the difference—if they can check and play defensive hockey. Hockey is the fastest team sport, and the fastest part of it is how quickly the puck can move from one team to the other, and back again.

From now on, you never have to feel left out of the game. You can be involved all the time, whether you have the puck or not. All you need is to be able to see what is happening on the ice and the ability to get into position to make the check. (These skills happen to be useful when you *have* the puck, too.) Learn good defensive skills, and your team will have the puck more of the time.

The basic idea of *Win with Defense* is this: Every player on the ice with the team that doesn't have the puck is a defender. That means every player can benefit from the inside tips in this book. Only a few players are scoring threats, but every player on a team that doesn't have the puck can be useful. You need to know what you bring to the game; it might be your defensive skills. That's an important lesson in itself.

The art of defense in this book is not divided by positions. At the age level the *Hockey the NHL Way* series is intended for, you are encouraged to play all the positions. Read this book, and you will know the game better. That will help you play any position.

Inside you'll find the so-called "little things" the pros say they have to do to win. They can be big things if you are a player who wants to rise to the top.

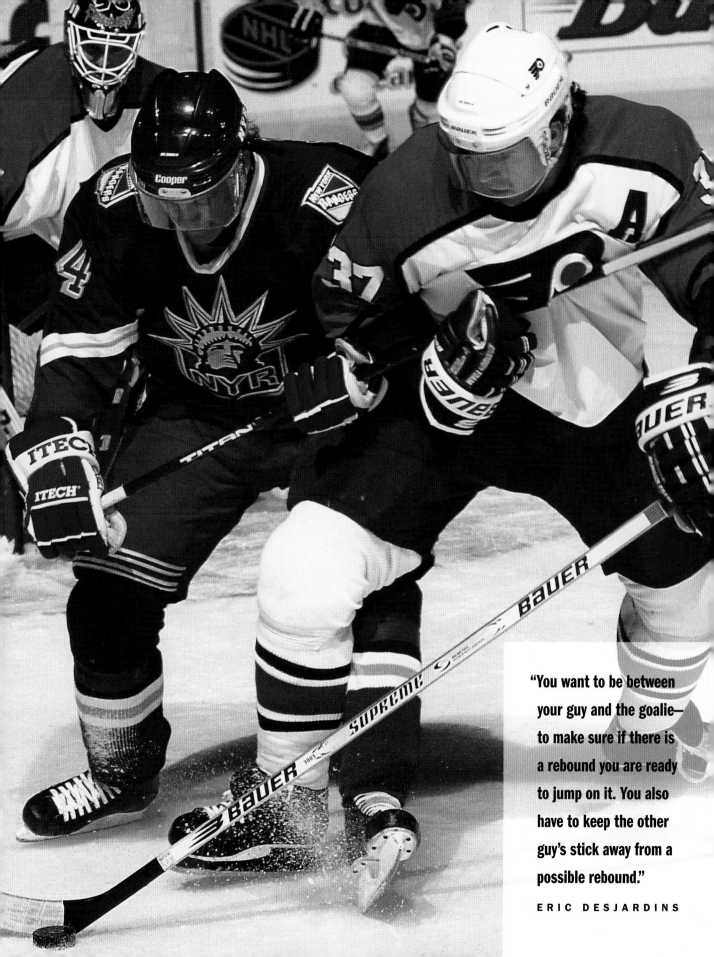

"You want to be between your guy and the goalie— to make sure if there is a rebound you are ready to jump on it. You also have to keep the other guy's stick away from a possible rebound."

ERIC DESJARDINS

You can't be a good checker unless you are a good skater. Why? Because you have to be able to stick to the puck carrier like glue if you want to take the puck away. The puck carrier always has the first move. You must react. You want to be the puck carrier's mirror image—the puck carrier's shadow. Give the puck carrier nowhere to hide.

Speed alone is not the ticket. It is better to be quick and agile—to be able to move in any direction, stop, start and back up—and to keep your feet moving all the time. Good checkers never stop until they get the puck.

Remember, how well you skate makes all the difference—between being an average player, and a great one.

S K A

TING

The first steps

Quickness is more important than sheer speed in hockey. The first few steps you take usually determine who gets to loose pucks first. Those first few steps should be short, driving, explosive steps, like a sprinter leaving the starting blocks.

- Have your feet close together, toes out.
- Dig the toes of your blades into the ice, knees well bent, and drive. Chop! Chop! Chop!
- Keep your upper body relaxed. Driving your arms forward can add power to a quick start.
- After your first few chops, begin to lengthen your stride.
- Push off hard on each stride so your blades make a rasp sound.

Lengthening your stride

The longer your stride, the less energy you need to get where you're going. Lean forward from the waist. Extend each stride as far to the side and back as possible. At the end of

Getting started

Will has his heels close together, toes out, knees bent, leaning forward.

He starts off with short, choppy steps, driving off the forward inside edge.

After five or six chops, he lengthens his stride and keeps his head up.

your power stroke, your back foot should be as square as possible to the direction you're moving in.

Concentrate on extending each stride as far as possible. Meanwhile, bend the front leg—the glide leg—to keep your body low to the ice. By bending the glide leg, you give it a more powerful thrust when it becomes the stride leg.

Crossovers

Use crossovers to add power and speed as you turn. You can begin practising crossovers by walking on the ice, following one of the faceoff circles. Simply lift your outside skate over the inside one, and transfer your weight to the new inside skate. Return the outside skate to its original position, and repeat.

Skating backward

Skating backward is easier than most people think. Just so you can feel better about trying it, start next to the boards. Grab the boards if you feel yourself falling.

Start skating backward by swinging one hip out and making a C-shaped cut in front and to the side as you move backward. Glide with the other foot. Continue to make C-cuts with each foot, one after another. You're skating backward!

Try to generate power by thrusting hard against the front inside edge of the skate you are making C-shaped cuts with.

T I P
As you try crossing over while gliding, remember to lean forward and into the turn for balance.

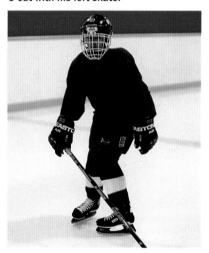
Jordan swings his left hip and begins a C-cut with his left skate.

He finishes the C-cut and is already shifting weight to his right leg.

He is about to begin the right-side C-cut and is moving backward, under control.

Skating better

Skating tips

- Keep low to the ice. Thrust hard with your back leg.
- Your upper leg muscles should feel the strain. That's where power comes from.
- When speed is what you want, carry your stick with your top hand alone.

"A lot more skating and defensive zone responsibility is involved with playing centre. You have to cover both sides of the ice, down low, and back up your D-men."

JEREMY ROENICK

Keeping a solid base

Everything you do on your skates starts with a solid base where your blades meet the ice. This means:

- your head is up, your back is straight,
- your feet are shoulder-width apart,
- your knees are bent, and
- your weight is equal on both feet.

How to do it

If you have a solid base, you're ready to move in any direction. Easy to do when you're standing still, right? But it's a lot harder when you're skating at top speed. You must be able to dart sideways—either way—stop, and move that way again.
You must be able to attack the puck carrier by driving forward or contain the play by backing off—and go sideways from moving forward or backward.

The defender is ready to move to either side: knees bent, feet shoulder-width apart, square to the puck carrier. Stay relaxed. Look at the puck carrier's chest.

The whole body pivots and turns to pursue the puck carrier. Go hard.

Moving sideways

The secret is to keep your feet moving. When you coast or stop, changing direction is more difficult.

Remember: The puck carrier will move sideways. You have to be able to go where the puck carrier goes. Just being in the puck carrier's way is good defense. If the puck carrier can't get past you, he or she has to give up the puck—or you'll take it.

Practise these skating skills and you will be a jitterbug on ice, a roadrunner. You'll have quick feet. Your coach's eyes will pop, because you'll be taking the puck, not just waiting for someone to give it to you. You'll be stuck to the puck carrier and impossible to dodge.

Quick, tight turns

When the puck carrier turns, you turn. Learn to turn by leaning and turning your feet in the direction you want to go. Don't stop and turn. Don't cross over. Just go that way, then be ready to go the other way.

Quick stops

When the puck carrier stops, you stop. You have to be able to stop going forward or backward—in a flash. A one-foot stop

Agility

Nowhere to hide: By reacting fast, Scott denies Danny the up-ice route.

Cut off from moving up the ice, Danny turns into the corner...

... now Scott has him where he wants him—within easy reach.

(stopping with your weight on just one foot) allows you to switch directions with your next step. When you stop hard with both feet, keep your feet moving and be ready to go in a new direction.

Agility should keep you in position, but speed is what gets you back into the play when you fall behind.

The key to being a good backchecker is to keep your feet moving and always overtake the puck carrier. Don't just catch up. You want to get in front of your check.

"My speed allows me to jump into the play and to join in attacking the net. It also allows me to drop back and play my defensive game."

SCOTT NIEDERMAYER

Good basic skills and honest effort in every game and practice can make you a solid two-way player, like Igor Larionov.

Transition skating

A "transition" happens when the puck changes hands. "Trans" means move, or change. "Transit" means travel. When your opponents get the puck, you change and become a checker—in an instant. When that happens, you need to be going in the opposite direction, *now.*

Work on your transition skating when you skate the lines. Stop on your back foot, cross over with your front foot as you turn your body toward the middle of the rink, then start back with short, choppy strides until you reach full speed.

Sculling

The puck carrier is in your radar. Sculling is how you close the gap. Come at the puck on an angle, taking away one of the puck carrier's choices. Move toward the puck carrier. Stay under

Scott sees his team get the puck—and he stops dead in his tracks . . .

. . . he crosses over and goes hard in the other direction . . .

. . . or sculls, pushing off with his back foot, looking for the puck.

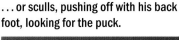

Changing gears

control: balanced, knees bent and feet shoulder-width apart. Push with your off-side foot—the foot away from your check—so that you're ready to go anywhere. Be square to the puck carrier.

Keep your stickblade on the ice. Most of the time, you'll protect the middle with your stick toward that side. Invite the puck carrier to move the puck along the boards.

Look at the puck carrier's body, not the puck or the puck carrier's head. Sculling is the way to close the gap and make the check.

The word "check" is a common term in hockey. Yet it's seldom used in other sports. Why? Because in no other sport does the thing everyone is chasing change hands so often, so quickly and in so many ways.

In hockey, everything changes when your team loses the puck or turns it over. You become a "checker." Instantly.

You have to find your "check." If your check has the puck, it is your job to perform one or more of a number of checks: stick-checks, poke-checks, or, when you are older, body checks. You backcheck, you forecheck. When your coach yells "Check-check-check," everybody knows what it means.

It means, "Get the puck."

CHE

MARTIN RUCINSKY & ERIC LINDROS▸

CKING

When you're the defensive player closest to the puck, positioning and angling help you attack the puck carrier.

Positioning

Positioning refers to where you should be on the ice. In your team's zone, for example, you should be between your check and the goal.

Angling

Angling is how you approach the puck carrier to get him or her to do what you want. For example: By angling toward the puck carrier from the middle toward the boards on a forecheck, you invite that player to pass the puck up the boards. Your teammate, following you on the forecheck and reading your angle, can figure out where your opponent's pass will go and be there, waiting for the puck to arrive.

Positioning & angling

The forechecker reads the defender's number. That means attack the puck. Go after it.

The defender has control of the puck. Contain. Play the pass.

Read-and-react

This is the time to read-and-react. If you're the first forechecker, you must read how well the puck carrier is controlling the puck. One key is the crest or number rule. The first forechecker reads the puck carrier: Do you see a sweater crest or number?

- If you see a crest, the puck carrier has control of the puck and has turned toward you. Contain.
- If you see a number, your opponent is trying to gain control of the puck. Attack.

Sizing up the play

What if you're the second forechecker? The second forechecker also reads and reacts. Don't rush into the play without thinking. You must size up the play deep in the offensive zone. If you're the second forechecker, here's what you look for:

- What angle is the first forechecker taking?
- Where is the first forechecker inviting the puck carrier to move the puck?
- Does the puck carrier have good control?
- Is the first forechecker attacking or containing?
- What kind of support does the puck carrier have? Are there teammates nearby?

These are the first signs that show you how the play will go. The second forechecker reads these signs and goes where the puck is most likely to go—before the puck is released.

N H L   T I P

"Give yourself evey opportunity to succeed—so you don't have regrets later."

S C O T T   S T E V E N S

The second forechecker goes where the pass was sent, takes control of the puck and looks for a third teammate in front of the net.

Meanwhile, the passer is eliminated by forechecker number one.

Positioning & angling

Putting it together

This is where teamwork comes in. The second forechecker must read what his or her teammate is inviting the puck carrier to do, and react by going where the puck is likely to go. If the first forechecker can take the puck or if that second player can intercept the pass, the two forecheckers, working together, will have a good chance to score.

Defense to offense—in a split second!

You are now close to the puck carrier on the forecheck, or the puck carrier is coming at you in your own zone. This is the moment to take the puck.

Poke-check

This is the best move to use when the puck carrier is approaching you head-on. Hold your stick with your top hand only, and thrust directly at the puck, with your stickblade flat on the ice. Don't lose your balance.

Sweep-check

This check works best from in front or slightly to one side against a good stickhandler. Instead of poking directly at the puck, sweep your stick low to the ice so it hits the puck carrier's stick.

Stick-checks

Poke-check. Go right at the puck, top hand on the stick, head up.

Sweep-check: Covers more ice, and forces the puck carrier to get rid of the puck.

T I P
Be very careful not to lift your opponent's stick above waist level. This is how many stick-related injuries occur.

Stick lift

Use a stick lift when approaching an opposing puck carrier from behind or at an angle. Move your lower hand down your stick for leverage. Lift your opponent's stick from low on the shaft, skate through the puck, and pick it up with your back skateblade.

Stick press

The opposite of lifting your opponent's stick. Just use your stick to press your opponent's stick down. Aim for the blade-to-handle joint.

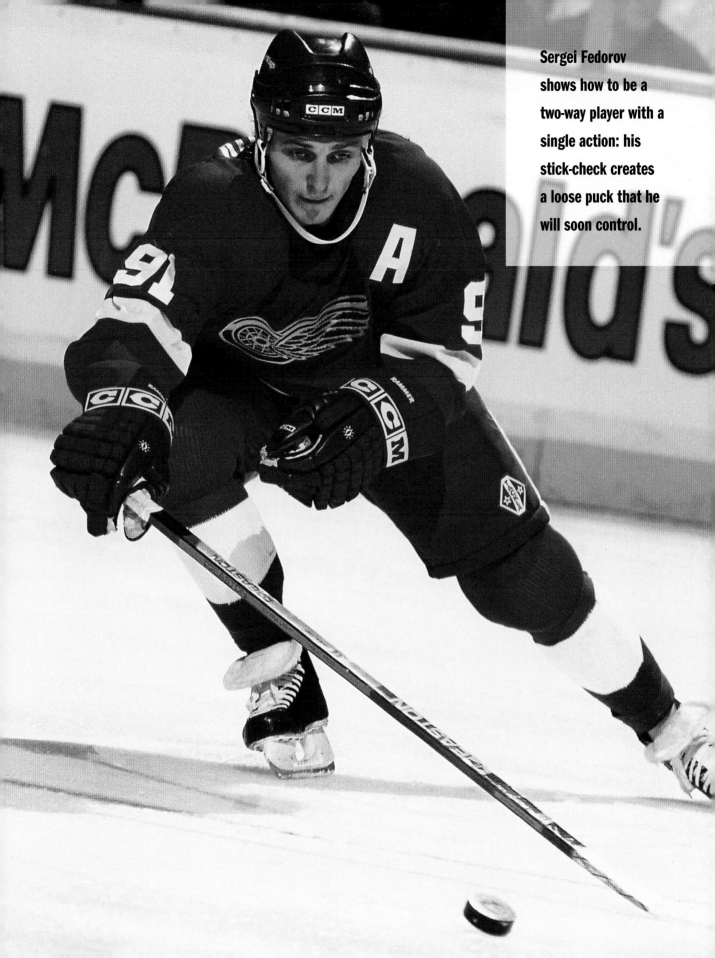

Sergei Fedorov shows how to be a two-way player with a single action: his stick-check creates a loose puck that he will soon control.

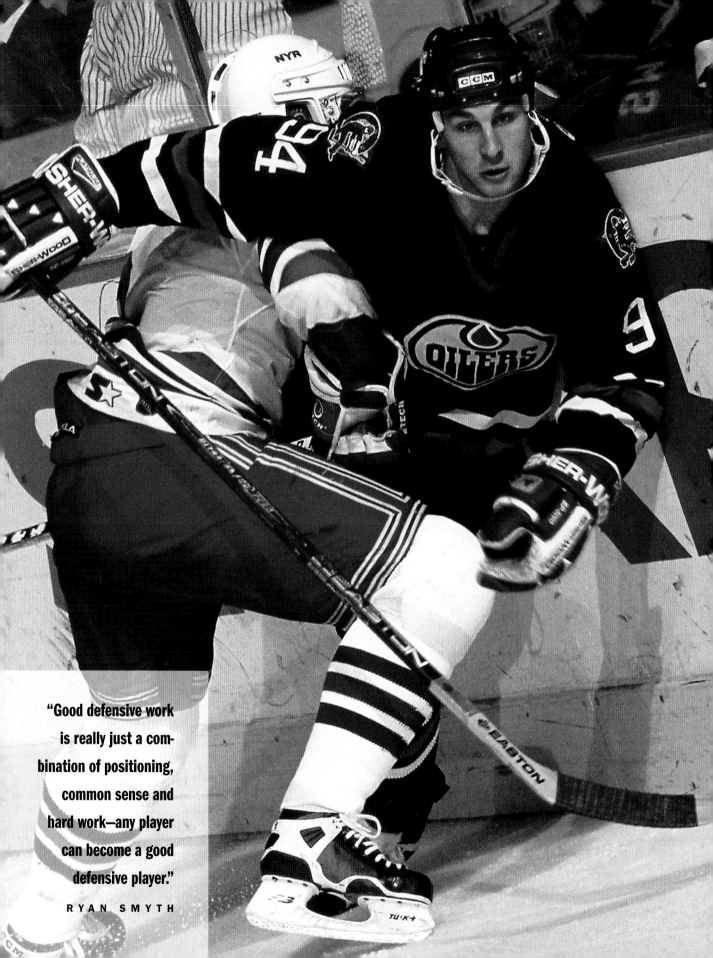

"Good defensive work
is really just a com-
bination of positioning,
common sense and
hard work—any player
can become a good
defensive player."

RYAN SMYTH

Body checking may not be allowed at your playing level. But body contact *will* take place when 10 kids, all of them after one puck, are skating in a confined area. The ability to make legal contact is an important skill in hockey. It is also a good way to prepare yourself for full-contact hockey in a few years' time.

Blocking the way

It is legal for a defender to block the way of the puck carrier— as long as the defender is in the lane first. You can not step into the puck carrier's path.

In your own zone, getting between your check and the net is your first task. If your check gets the puck and you are in position, you will be blocking the way. This is hard to do. But being in the puck carrier's way makes you a good defensive player.

T I P

It is important to learn how to control offensive players without hitting them, no matter what level of hockey you are playing. Good defensive skills are often the key to moving up to the next level.

The checker can simply skate the puck carrier off the puck and take control.

Leaning into the puck carrier along the boards is legal . . .

. . . and so is simply stepping between the puck carrier and the puck.

Body contact

Leaning into the puck carrier

If you and the puck carrier are going in the same direction, you can lean into him or her. You may even be able to deflect the puck carrier from his or her path. Keep your feet moving to stay with the puck carrier. To prevent a penalty, do not hook or hold your opponent.

When body checking is not allowed, you can not finish a check by running the puck carrier into the boards. In fact, you can't check anyone but the puck carrier.

Once you develop quick feet and learn how to angle in on the puck carrier, you perform these skills without thinking. The next step is to *combine* your skating and checking skills, so that you are using them together at the right times.

This is where you really learn the game of hockey from the inside out. When NHL players talk about winning by doing the little things right, they're talking about being in position and knowing who to check.

There are certain plays that happen again and again during games. You can learn to read those plays and react the right way—every time.

Make playing solid defense a habit. It can be just as much fun as scoring goals, and you can do it more often.

THE INS

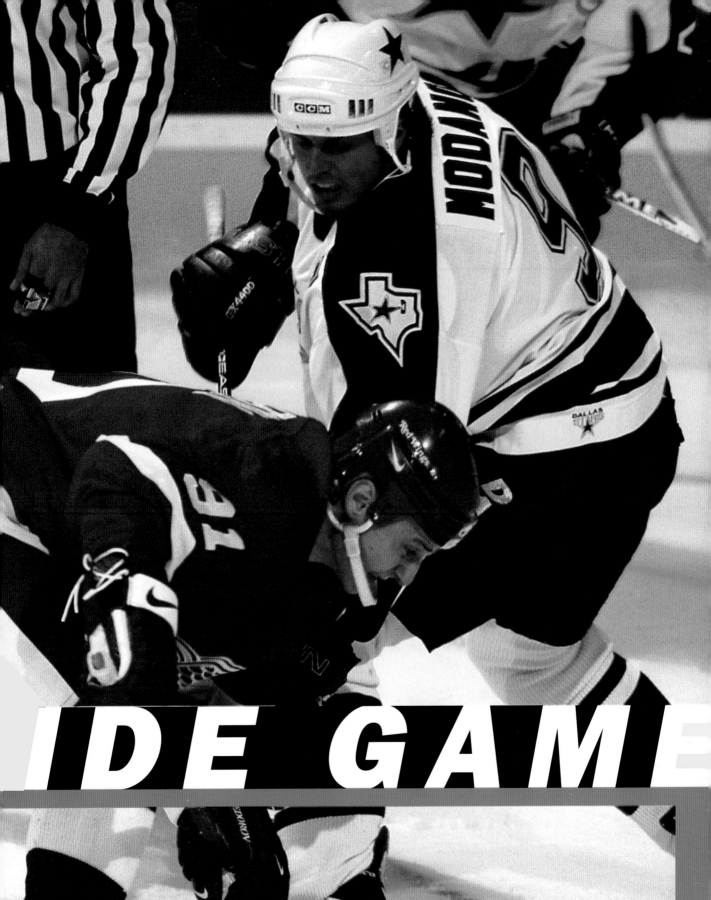

IDE GAME

We are calling these actions skills, because they require practise to learn. But you will want to make them habits.

Head on a swivel

First, you have to see what's happening to be able to read the play. Be aware at all times of where everyone is. You probably do this when you are skating toward a loose puck, so you'll know what to do when you get there. But make it a habit all the time.

Quick feet

Second, you have to be in position to make the check. To do that, always maintain your momentum. Keep your feet moving, never coast. When you lose the puck, stop, turn the other way and go get it back.

Reading the play

The puck carrier comes from behind the net at full speed, with good puck control. Don't commit. Contain.

The puck carrier is coming at you hard. Maintain the gap. Back off.

Read-and-react

There is no one play that shows all the ways to read-and-react on the ice. Reading and reacting to what's going on around you is more than a skill you'll use in just a few situations. It's a way of being more aware of the game and your part in it—all the time.

Reading and reacting is a better way to play hockey. It's a skill that will make you a better player anywhere on the ice. An example of a read-and-react skill is reading the gap between you and the puck carrier.

The gap is the amount of space between you and the play. Controlling the size of the gap between you and the puck gives you an edge: you can invite the puck carrier to do what you want by deciding whether to attack the puck or hold off and contain. Remember: The key question is, should I attack or contain?

Read the gap

The smaller the gap between you and the puck carrier, the higher the risk of the puck carrier going around you—and the better your chance of making the check. The closer you are to the puck the more you're at risk, and the more you're committed to making the check. Whether you move in to attack or back off and contain depends on how well the puck carrier is controlling the puck, and on how much support you have from your teammates.

T I P

Controlling the gap is one way to put pressure on the puck carrier—or to take pressure off.

As Nicolas slows up, he closes the gap, inviting Danny to go outside.

When Danny reads the wide gap, he could choose to cut across in front of Nicolas. Nicolas must move sideways to defend.

Gap control

The bigger the gap, the more time and space the puck carrier has to make a play. You must be ready to go in any direction.

Remember: By controlling the size of the gap between you and the puck, you invite the puck carrier to do what you want.

Read the gap checklist

- **Close the gap:** You force the puck carrier to beat you one-on-one or to get rid of the puck quickly.
- **Open the gap:** You invite the puck carrier to try to make a play.

You know *what* gap control is, but how do you know *when* to attack and when to contain? Answer: It depends on how well the puck carrier is controlling the puck.

■ If your opponent has poor puck control, go hard for the puck.
■ If your opponent has good puck control, back off and contain.

What if you're skating toward an opponent who is going for a loose puck?

■ If you can see the player's number, attack the puck.
■ If you can see the player's sweater crest, contain.

Why? If you can see the player's number, your opponent has his or her back to you and is still picking up the puck. Attack. (Don't bump your opponent into the boards. Approach at an angle.)

Attack or contain?

The opponent turns toward the boards to pick up the puck. Attack, but be careful of the boards.

Your opponent has control. You see the crest. Contain.

T I P
Gap control is a tool you can use anywhere on the ice—except near your own net.

But if you can see the player's crest, that means your opponent has control, has turned around with the puck and is looking to make a play. Contain.

Attack or contain checklist

■ Is the puck carrier coming at you hard? Back off, contain, and keep yourself in the play.
■ Are you outnumbered? Contain and try to prevent the pass. Stall for time until help arrives from your teammates.
■ Is the puck carrier having problems handling the puck? Attack.

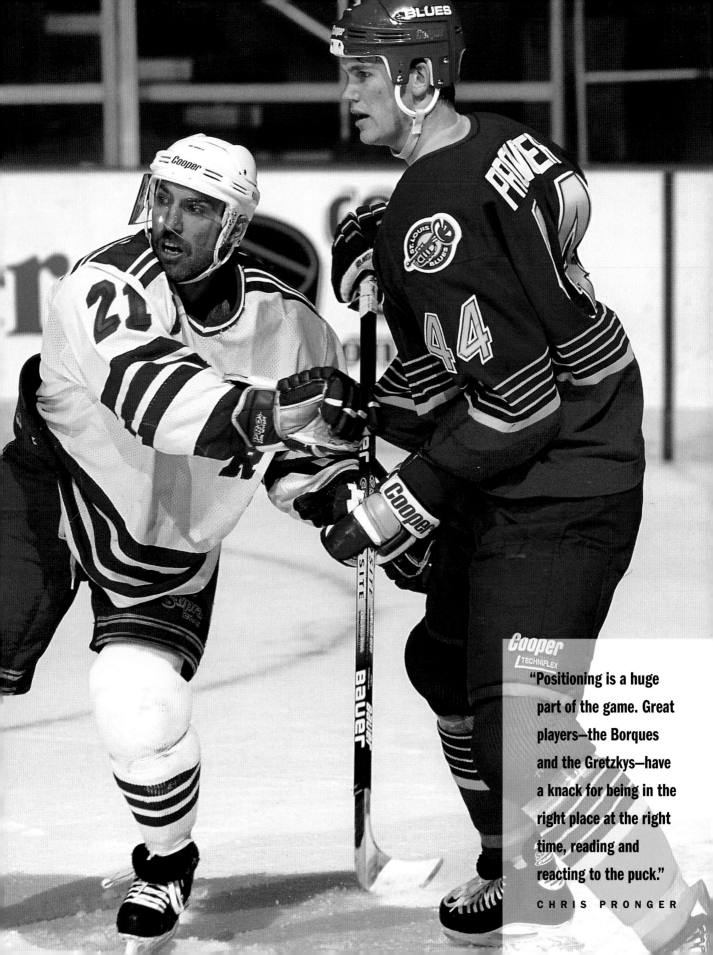

What is the mid-ice lane?

The mid-ice lane runs up and down the ice surface from goalmouth to goalmouth and between the faceoff dots. The team that has the puck has to move it into the lane in front of its opponents' goal to have the best chance of scoring. The defensive team tries to keep the puck out of that lane—out along the boards.

When you think about it, this only makes sense. On a power play, the penalty killers allow the puck to move around the outside of their defensive zone. They also work hard to keep it out of the slot, or shooting zone.

So hockey is played within three marked zones, and inside and outside an unmarked zone. The marked zones are contained by the bluelines, which run from side to side. The unmarked zone—the mid-ice lane—runs the length of the ice, from goal line to goal line.

The mid-ice lane

Always keep the mid-ice lane in mind when defending. Inside the lane, at either end, attack the puck. Outside, contain.

The defender is playing on the shooter's inside shoulder, inviting him or her to go outside.

Controlling the mid-ice lane

You must be aware of this unmarked zone to play defensive hockey well. Most of the dangerous scoring chances in a game are created here. The more you can keep the attacking team out of the mid-ice lane, the fewer goals you are likely to give up.

This is the battle that goes on as long as the game lasts. Every time you decide whether to attack the puck or contain the puck carrier, your decision will depend partly on where the puck is

within this invisible zone that runs the length of the ice.
Remember, when the other team has the puck:

- control play in the mid-ice lane, and
- force your opponents to shoot from outside.

Playing the mid-ice lane

Think about this end-to-end zone when your opponents have the
puck—no matter where you are on the ice. Attack the puck if
the puck carrier is in front of your net—or your opponents' net.

Always attack the puck if it's near the net—either net. Both
of these areas are within the mid-ice lane.

If your opponent has good control of the puck, you might want
to try and keep him or her along the boards. Your opponent is
not dangerous there. Try to block a pass into the middle, where
your opponents are more of a threat.

N H L T I P
"When I work harder at those one-on-one battles I get the puck
more often. I don't wait for the puck, I go after it. My defense
creates my offense."
M I K E M O D A N O

Front of the net: watch the puck, stay in touch with your check.

Head on a swivel: stickblade on the ice, eyes on the receiver. That's your check.

The mid-ice lane

Mid-ice checklist

- Give your opponents the outside—deny them the middle.
- Attack the puck at either net.
- Block passes into the middle.
- Stay on the inside of your check.
- When the other team has the puck, protect the mid-ice lane.
  Keep your opponents out of this lane, and they're less
  likely to score.

In hockey, you make decisions about what to do several times in a single shift. What you do depends on where you are on the ice.

Your defensive zone is the Danger Zone. This is where you must stay alert, read the play and react the fastest. Making a check near your own goal can be as satisfying as scoring a goal—it is just as important.

The rules are simple. Stay between your check and the net. Look for the puck. Keep your stick on the ice. Protect the middle.

One good thing about defending in your own zone is that you know where your opponents are trying to put the puck. Wait long enough, be in the right place, and the puck will come to you.

THE DEF

KELLY BUCHBERGER

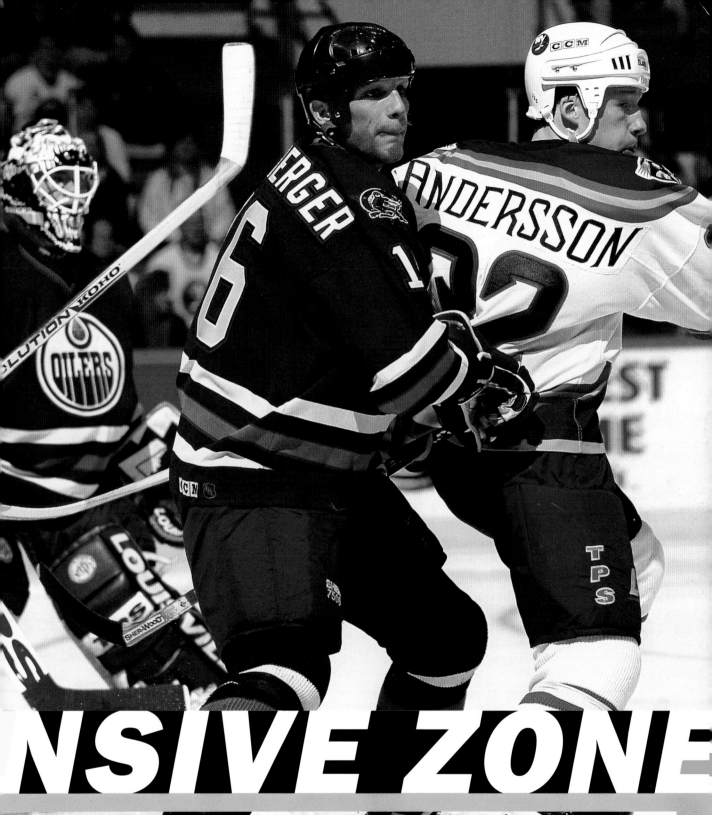

NSIVE ZONE

Positioning

The first rule of defending in your own zone is to pick up your check and stay between that player and the net.

Most of the time, just being with your check will eliminate him or her from the play. But don't just shadow your check. Look around. Keep in touch. Use your stick to feel where your check is as you look away for the puck.

Leave your check only when you see your chance to take the puck. Be 100 per cent sure. If there is any doubt, stay in position rather than going for the puck.

Pressure or contain?

More than anywhere else on the ice, in your own zone you want to go after the puck when your check has it. If you take the puck your team's problem is solved. Miss, and things go from bad to worse.

The danger zone

Pass from the corner: eyes on the puck, stick on your opponent's stick.

The puck carrier skates out of the corner. Stay with your check, let the goalie take the shooter.

T I P

In your own zone, if you stay in position the puck may come to you.

So it has to be controlled pressure. That means there are times when you should contain instead of pressuring.

For example, when the puck carrier is coming out of the corner and has a teammate in the slot, the puck carrier has two options: go to the net, or pass. You must contain. Do your job, and stay with your check. This forces the puck carrier to go to the net. Let your goalie take the shooter.

When to contain

- When you're the last line of defense.
- When missing the check would give your opponent a scoring chance. Let the puck carrier come to you. A good example is when the puck carrier comes out of the corner. Missing the check would put the puck carrier alone in front of the net. So back off. Stay between him or her and the net.
- When you're outnumbered near your own net. Again, don't take yourself out of the play by going for the puck. Let the goalie take the puck carrier. Stay between your opponents and play the pass.

When to attack

Sooner or later, the play will come close to your net and you will have to pressure the puck carrier. Force the puck carrier to make a good pass or take a shot on goal.

T I P

Don't panic. Just because your opponents have the puck in your zone doesn't mean they'll score. Stay cool. Cover your check and wait for the puck to come your way.

Covering the point: face your check, eyes on the puck.

Player covering in front only goes for the puck when 100 per cent sure of taking possession.

The danger zone

- Don't leave your feet—that will take you out of the play. Don't try to deflect an incoming shot. Let your goalie see the puck.
- If your team is running around, try to get a whistle. Freeze the puck against the boards. Fall on it if you can. Ice the puck, or at least get it out of the zone.
- When they score, don't blame anyone else. Don't bang your stick on the ice. Stay cool.

Controlling your opponent

Any player might have to cover the front of your team's net. This is where you can make the difference between the other team scoring or your team taking the puck in the other direction. This is where the puck will arrive, sooner or later.

Just being with your check in the slot is not enough. You have to know where the puck is and control your opponent in different ways, depending on where the shot will come from. Your head is on a swivel. You look from the puck to your check, and back again.

Read-and-react

If the puck is in the corner: Stay between your check and the puck. That means watching for the pass but staying in touch with your check. Leave your check only when you are 100 per cent sure the puck is yours.

In front of the net

The defender has good net-side coverage of the most dangerous player—the one in front of the net. Goalie takes the shooter.

T I P

In front of the net, think rebound. Anticipate where the rebound will go and be there first.

If the puck is at the point: You need to do two things. First, stay in contact with your check. Know the path your check wants to take and block that path. If your opponent is screening the goalie's view, move him or her out of the way.

Second, when the shot comes, control your check's stick. Lift it to prevent a deflection and to keep your check from scoring on a rebound.

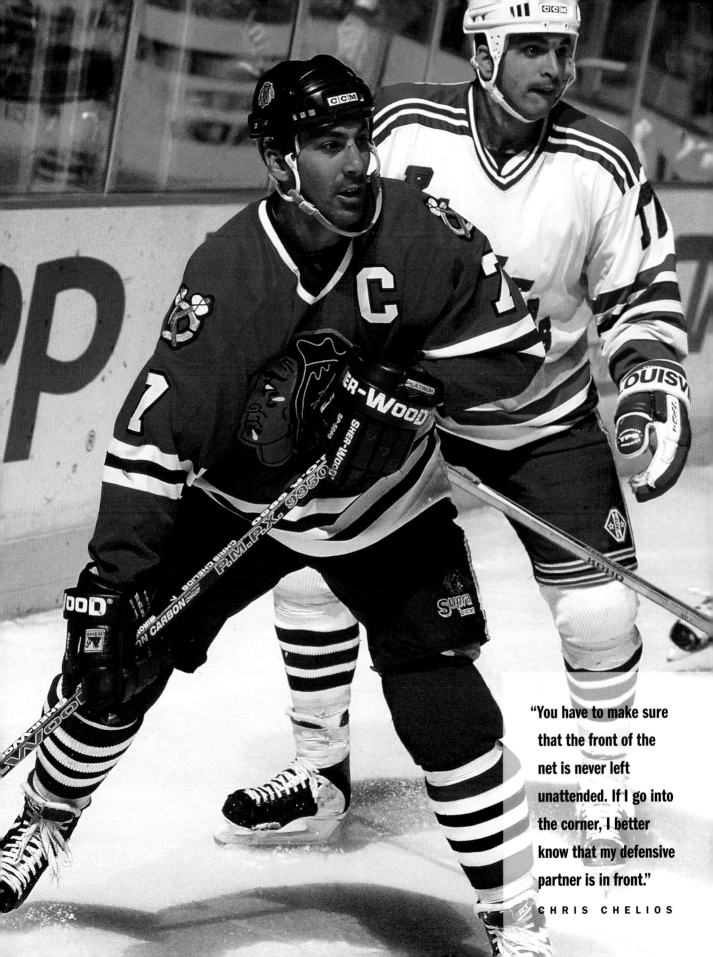

"You have to make sure
that the front of the
net is never left
unattended. If I go into
the corner, I better
know that my defensive
partner is in front."

CHRIS CHELIOS

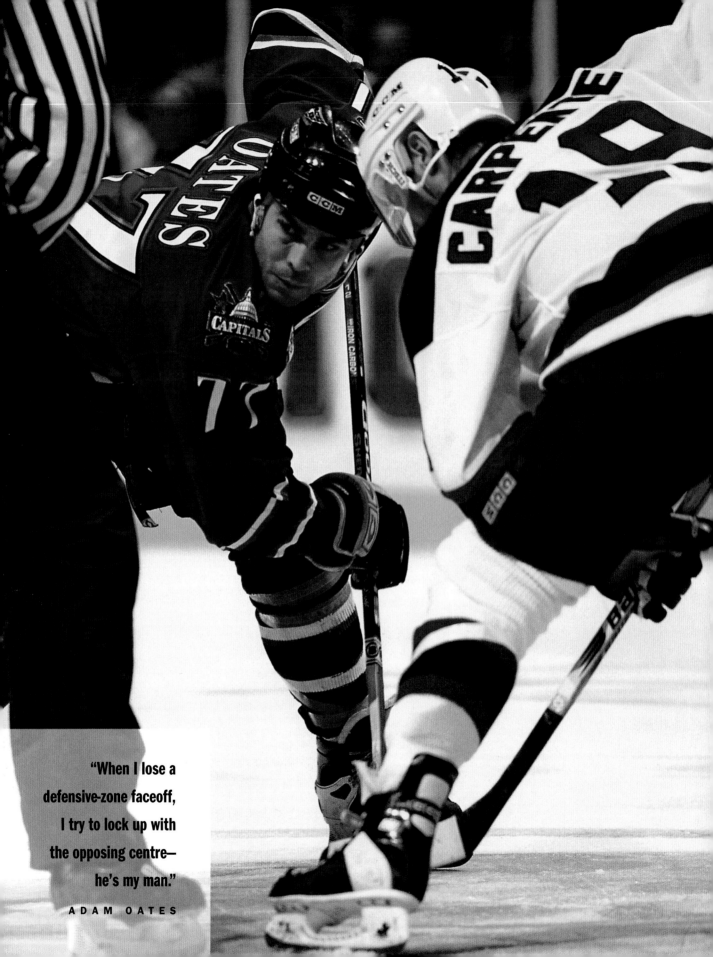

"When I lose a
defensive-zone faceoff,
I try to lock up with
the opposing centre—
he's my man."
ADAM OATES

Any stick-to-stick action creates danger. *You* are to blame for any damage your stick causes when you are doing anything other than handling the puck. Be careful with your stick. It is most useful when the blade is on the ice.

- Never carry your stick high. The puck moves on the ice; you can't play it with your stick in the air. But you can hurt someone badly when you carry your stick high.

- Never use the butt end of your stick on an opponent.

- Never push an opponent from behind along the boards. Observe a 4-foot/1.2-m safety zone along the boards.

- Never bump an opponent within the 4-foot/1.2-m safety zone. Play the *puck* along the boards, not the player.

A high stick hurts your opponent, your team, or both. Don't take the risk.

Butt-ending is a cheap shot that can cost you big time in penalties.

Hitting from behind can leave your opponent paralyzed for life.

The nevers of defensive play

How things go in your own zone depends on how they went in the neutral zone. Problems in the neutral zone become scoring chances at your net.

The neutral zone is where a smart defender can really shine. By hustling back to help you can even up the odds when your team is outnumbered at your blueline. Skate hard coming back, and your coach will be sure to notice. Just by being with your check, you allow your defense to play on the blueline rather than backing in.

When the defense is able to stand up and play on the blueline, two good things can happen for your team. A cross-ice pass will end up on a defender's stick or an opponent will be forced to go off-side. Either way, the rush is over.

THE NE

AL MacINNIS ▶

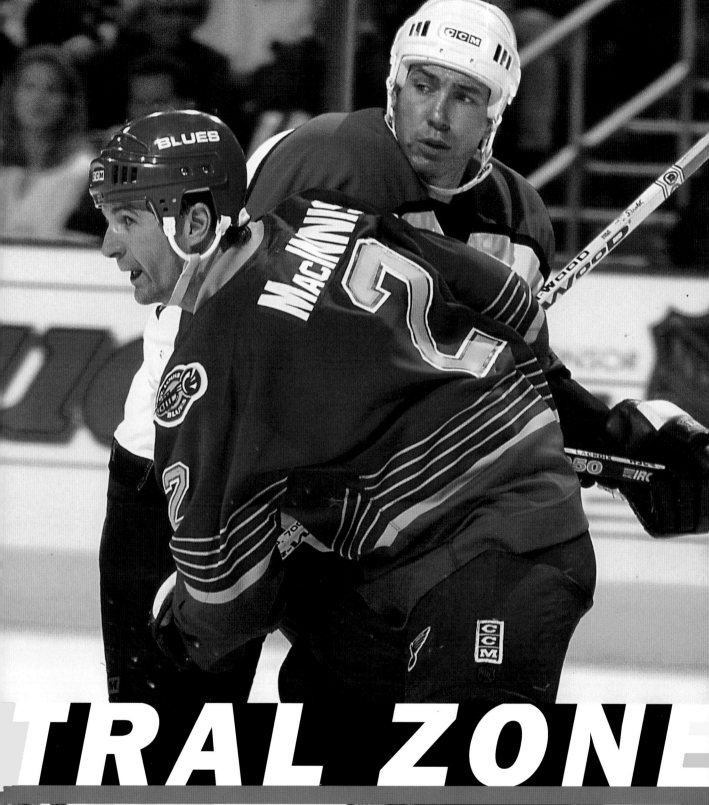

TRAL ZONE

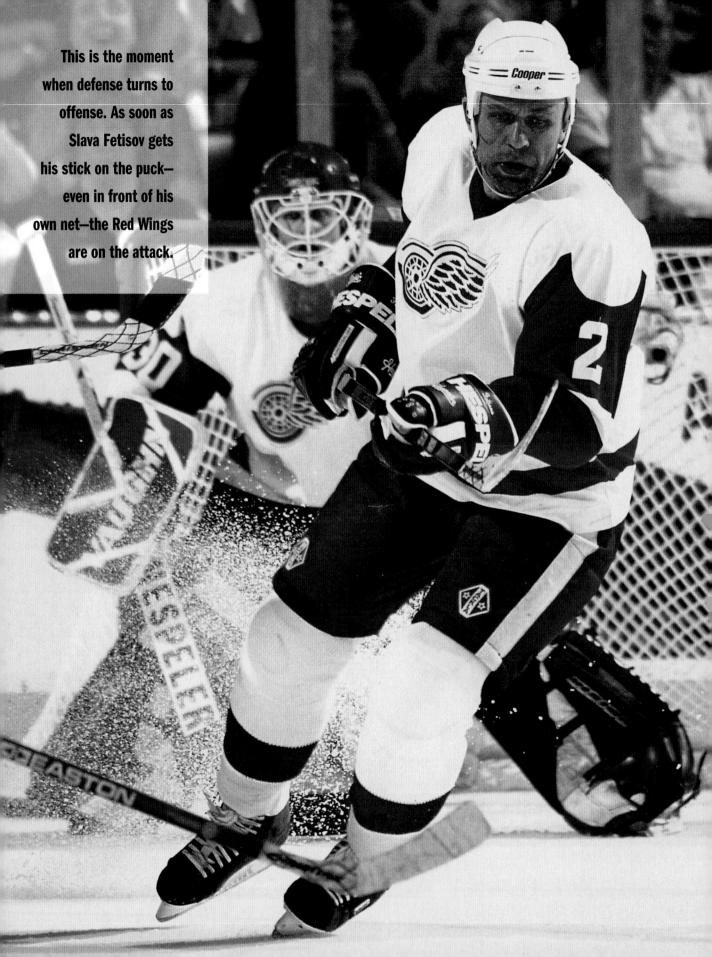

This is the moment when defense turns to offense. As soon as Slava Fetisov gets his stick on the puck—even in front of his own net—the Red Wings are on the attack.

The other team has the puck and they're coming at you. What do you do? Look to see who has the edge. Is your team outnumbered? Do you have a numbers advantage, or are the numbers even?

How to do it

If the numbers are even: If it's one-on-one, two-on-two or three-on-three, take the player nearest you. Stay with your check. If your check is the puck carrier, make sure he or she loses control of the puck. Always protect the middle. Remember: On even-numbered plays, you still have the advantage. Win each of the one-on-ones and you win the five-on-five.

If the defense outnumbers the attackers: Immediately pressure the puck carrier. If the puck carrier is your check or the player closest to you, take him or her. Block his or her way to the net. Don't worry about the puck.

> **T I P**
> Watch for two attackers to criss-cross to disrupt your coverage. When that happens, stay with your check.

Two-on-two. The defender nearest to the puck can attack the shooter, because his teammate has eliminated the other forward.

Playing the rush

If you're outnumbered: If the play is two-on-one, three-on-one or three-on-two, try to stall the attack until help comes. Allow moves to the outside, deny passes into the middle. Let the goaltender take the puck carrier. Remember, the key points are:
- Stall. Take the inside position between the play and your net. Contain your opponent.
- Defend the middle. Deny passes into the slot. Let the goaltender take the shot.

Even when you don't have the puck, there is one aspect of the attack you can control: the gap between you and the play. By playing tight to the play or loose, a few steps away, you are telling the puck carrier what to do.

How to do it

When you play tight: This means you invite the puck carrier to beat you. Play tight when the numbers are even or better, and when you feel confident the puck carrier can't beat you.

When you play loose: Leave a larger gap, and you invite the puck carrier to turn sideways or make a play. Keep a wide gap when you're outnumbered, or when the puck carrier has good control.

Remember: Playing the gap in the neutral zone is like deciding whether to attack or contain the puck carrier, except that you read-and-react to a play that involves several players.

Playing the gap

Nicolas plays the puck carrier tight, forcing his opponent to pass or go around him.

Outnumbered? Keep a loose gap. Brian wants to prevent a pass to Kellin in the middle.

Heads up

Watch for the rink-wide pass. On the rush, the most dangerous players are the ones away from the puck.

When your team is guarding its blueline well and trying to check the opposition outside your defensive zone, the puck carrier has two choices: a rink-wide pass or a shot into your zone. Both can result in your team getting the puck back. A rink-wide pass at your blueline can be a turnover if you're expecting it.

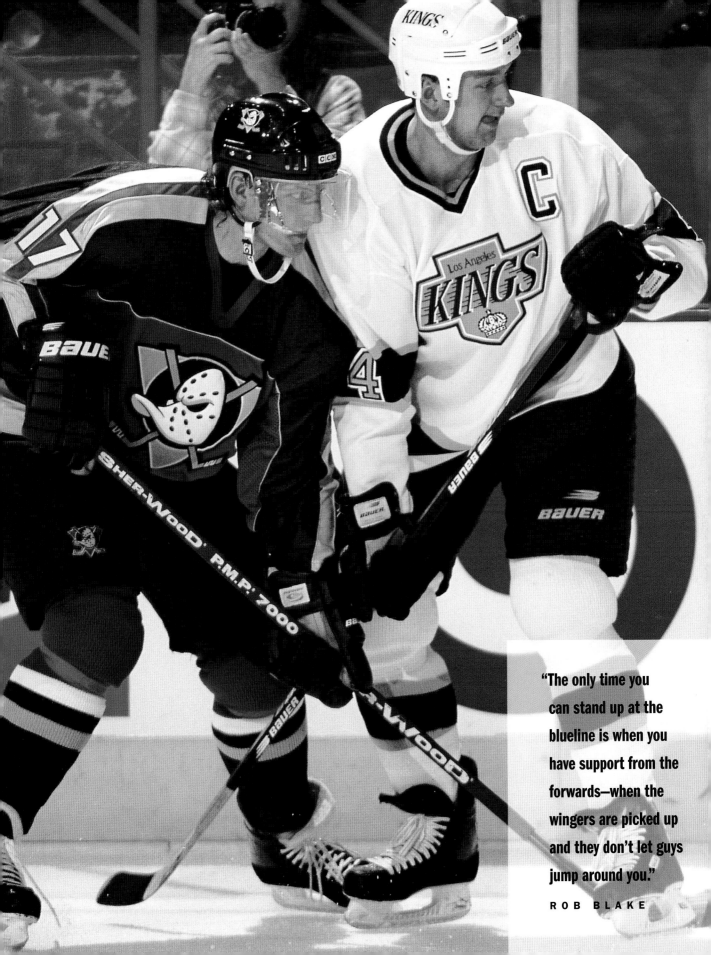

"The only time you can stand up at the blueline is when you have support from the forwards—when the wingers are picked up and they don't let guys jump around you."

ROB BLAKE

Defense to offense

Intercepting a rink-wide pass outside your own blueline is one of the many ways you can start a lightning-quick turnaround in the neutral zone.

The whole idea of playing good defense is to get the puck and move it in the other direction. If you can do it when your opponents are skating hard into your zone, that's even better. You can catch them going the wrong way.

As soon as you have the puck at your own blueline, look up-ice for a teammate coming back late. Put the puck on his or her stick and the result may be a breakaway.

So don't wait. Look for the quick pass first or carry the puck yourself. Get going in the other direction!

Transition

The blue team has lost the puck. Danny, in red, reads the play and looks for a pass . . .

Scott slams on the brakes, eyeballs the play, and starts in the other direction. He is already in a position to intercept a pass to Danny.

Stay with your check

If your team loses the puck in the neutral zone you become an instant defender. Don't coast in a big circle. Stop, then find your check. Place yourself between your check and the puck.

If your check has the puck, you're probably nearby and in a position to make the check. So stop dead, turn around and go for the puck. In the neutral zone, you are likely to be skating in the same direction as your check. This is the ideal position for making stick-checks.

Reading and reacting

Almost everything you do while defending in the neutral zone involves reading and reacting. The difference in the neutral zone is that you're reading the big picture.

What to look for

- Are you outnumbered? If so, is help from your team on the way?
- Are they coming hard, with good puck control? Offer them a wide gap and stay in the play.
- Protect the middle. Allow your opponents to go wide but deny the pass into the mid-ice lane.
- Look for the rink-wide pass at the blueline. It's your chance to turn defense into offense in a split second.

N H L   T I P

"The biggest thing about being a forward and playing defensively is to be aware of who's on the ice—aware of who's in front of you. Stay low and help the defense."

D O U G   G I L M O U R

The tables are turned: The blue team gets the puck. Scott looks for the pass and Danny must react.

Danny has two strides to make up. He wants to get to Scott's inside shoulder to prevent a pass to Scott.

Transition

Be a quick-change artist

Good defensive players often score key goals in tight games. The key to making the most of a turnover is to strike fast—to catch your opponents skating the wrong way.

- If you have the puck, turn and look to make the quick pass.
- If you see the turnover happen, make yourself available for a pass. One way to do that is to skate hard across the ice, so your teammate with the puck can spot you.
- Learn to take passes from directly behind you.

Playing well defensively has many rewards, but none feel as good as taking the puck from your opponents in their own zone—and then scoring.

You have that chance when you forecheck hard in the offensive zone. Here, more than anywhere else on the ice, is where you cash in the fastest. So be aggressive. Go in hard. Make your opponents move the puck faster than they would like to. Sometimes, when they are rushed, they will put the puck on one of your teammate's sticks.

Your chances of scoring are better than on the rush because you'll be taking your opponents by surprise. One moment they have the puck and are starting the breakout. The next moment they are fishing it out of their own net.

THE OFFE

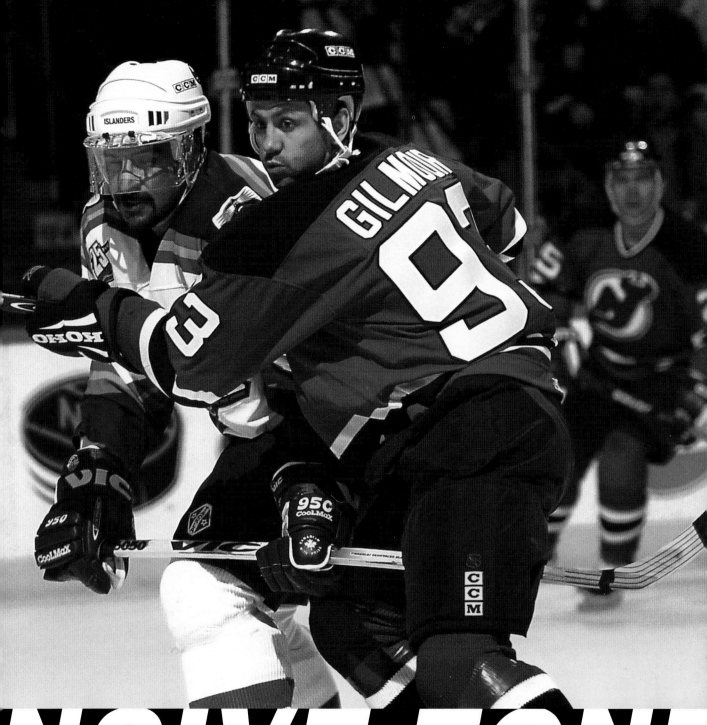

NSIVE ZONE

"Players sometimes forget that preventing goals is as important as scoring. I take a defense-first attitude in my approach to the game—every night."

MIKE PECA

Steering the play

As you know, the first forechecker into the offensive zone attacks the puck by approaching the puck carrier *at an angle*, denying the pass where the forechecker is coming from and inviting a pass in the other direction.

Sometimes the puck carrier will try to pass through the forechecker. That's the forechecker's chance to take the puck. But, more often, the puck carrier will take the invitation.

Pressure on the puck

Most of the time, it takes two players to steal the puck on the forecheck. The first forechecker steers the play. He or she approaches the puck carrier at an angle, such as coming from the slot toward the corner, to force the puck up the boards.

> **N H L T I P**
> "Special teams often decide the outcome of games. When my team is leading and it's late in the game, I take special pride in killing off a shorthanded situation."
> **K E L L Y   B U C H B E R G E R**

Forechecking takes teamwork. The first forechecker steers the play.

If you are the first forechecker, go hard for the puck. Make the puck carrier get rid of it.

Force the play

You want the puck carrier and your teammates to see where you are inviting your opponent to pass the puck. The second forechecker reads the direction open to the puck carrier to pass or go to, and goes there.

If the second forechecker sees his teammate angle in on the puck carrier from the middle, he knows the first forechecker is inviting the puck carrier to move the puck up the boards. Reading these cues tells the second forechecker to go to the boards.

The puck comes up the boards and bingo!—scoring chance.

Creating the turnover

Picking up a loose puck along the boards is one way to create turnovers in the offensive zone. But there are actually more ways to take control of the puck in your opponents' zone than anywhere else on the ice.

In the offensive zone, every forward should attack the puck hard. If you miss there will be a second chance. Always make sure your angle of attack takes away one option and invites another. If you have a choice, try to take away the mid-ice lane. Make your opponents move the puck along the boards. It is easier to keep the puck in your opponents' zone along the boards.

Get the puck

The second forechecker reads the teammate's angle of attack and anticipates where the puck will go . . .

. . . and goes to that spot, looking for a third teammate to pass to.

By forechecking hard, you press your opponents to make decisions faster than they want to. Often they will cough up the puck.

Each time a forechecker attacks the puck, he or she creates the chance for a turnover. Either the forechecker takes the puck or the teammate who is giving support goes where the puck is likely to go. Anticipate!

Finally, just playing most of the game in your opponents' zone can create turnovers. Players under pressure to make a quick play often hand the puck over to their opponents.

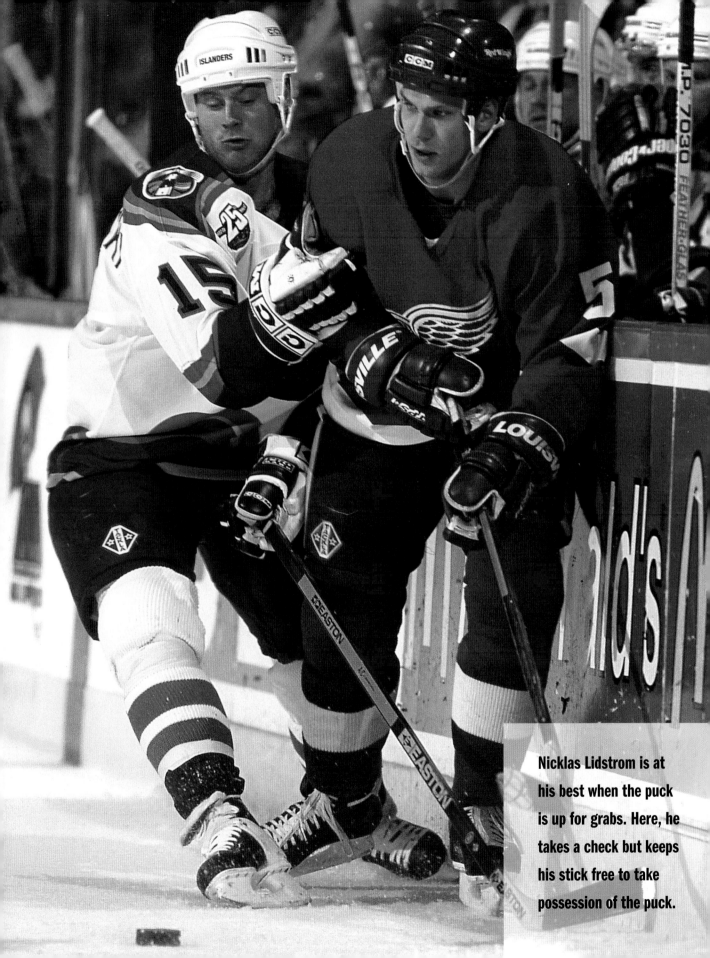

Nicklas Lidstrom is at his best when the puck is up for grabs. Here, he takes a check but keeps his stick free to take possession of the puck.

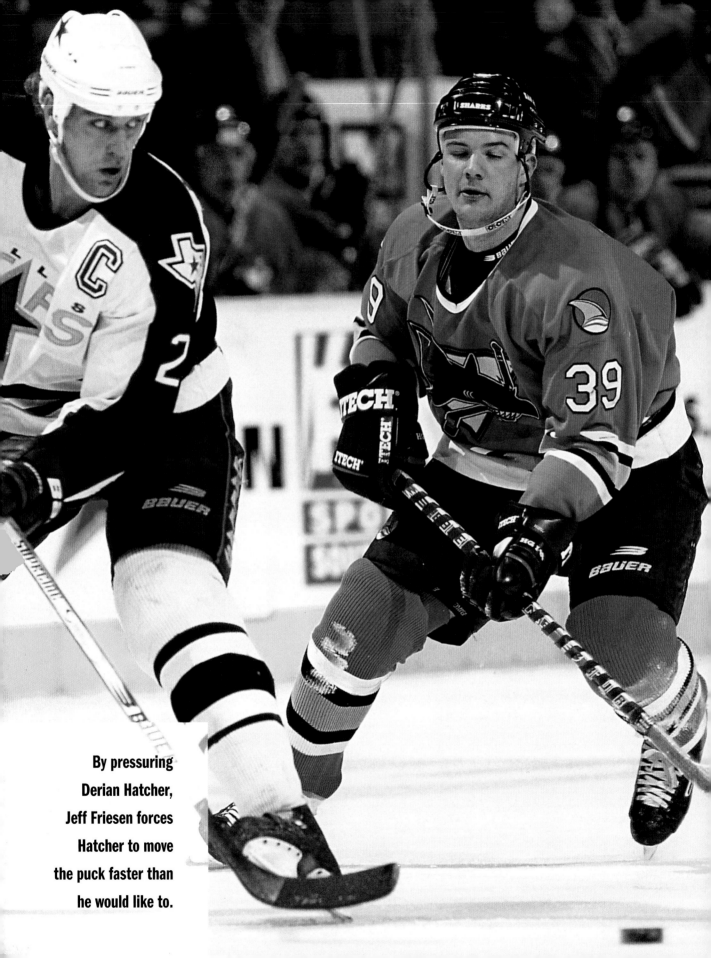

By pressuring Derian Hatcher, Jeff Friesen forces Hatcher to move the puck faster than he would like to.

Eliminate your check

The moment your team loses control of the puck in the offensive zone, don't be lazy. Look for your check and pick him or her up. Stay between your check and the puck to make sure they're not open for a pass. Just by being there, you keep your check from being part of your opponents' breakout. It's almost like making them play shorthanded.

If your check has the puck, be aggressive. Try to strip the puck before your check gets out of the zone. If you get control, shoot the puck deep into the zone.

Reading and reacting

Forechecking in the offensive zone is reading and reacting in its purest form.

TIP
Stay alert for the pass up the middle. Stealing the puck in the mid-ice lane of your opponents' zone is a defender's dream come true.

Kellin looks for a pass as Nicolas reacts to his team losing the puck . . .

. . . but Nicolas catches up as Kellin gains control, preventing a pass into the middle.

Keep control

The first forechecker into the zone reads whether the puck carrier has good control (by watching for the player's number or crest), and reacts by attacking the puck or by inviting the puck carrier to move the puck one way or the other.

The second player into the zone reads where the first forechecker is inviting the puck carrier to move the puck, and goes there.

Remember: Read the play to see where the puck will go, then react by going there in time to make a play.

Resources

There are few resources for players and coaches who want to learn the art of defense. Here are some that are available.

Videos

Right Start Beginning Checking, Skating, Puck Control
International Hockey Centre of Excellence
The Canadian Hockey Association has made a three-part video in its *Right Start* series; the first two parts deal with defensive hockey. *Right Start* is sold at the NHL arenas in Ottawa, Toronto, Calgary and Vancouver. You can also order it from:
The Canadian Hockey Association
607 – 1600 James Naismith Drive
Gloucester, Ontario   K1B 5N4
Phone: (613) 748-5613

Defense Concepts
International Hockey Centre of Excellence,
with George Kingston
Crudely made but crammed with individual and team defense techniques and drills (including a clear explanation of the mid-ice lane concept).

Goals 2: Read and React for Defensemen
International Hockey Centre of Excellence
Many of the ideas in *Win with Defense* are taught on this tape, including developing "quick feet," covering in front of the net and playing in the corners.

Hockey for Kids and Coaches
Can-Am Hockey Group
Features NHL stars giving tips on all aspects of hockey. Bob Gainey (backchecking), Rod Langway (defense) and Laura Stamm (power skating) offer their expertise.

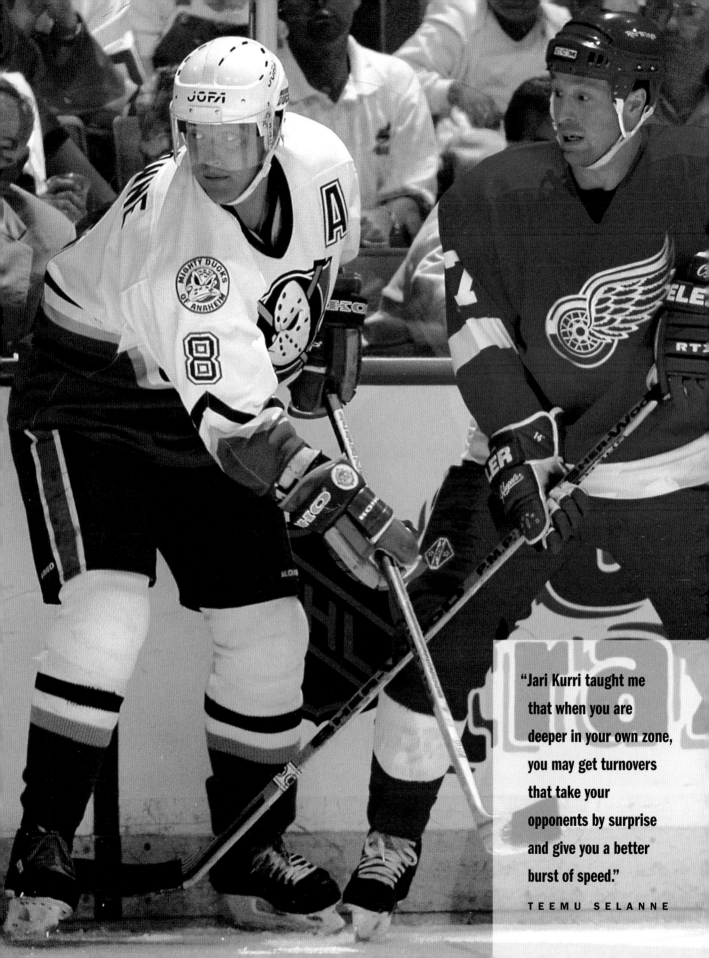

"Jari Kurri taught me that when you are deeper in your own zone, you may get turnovers that take your opponents by surprise and give you a better burst of speed."

TEEMU SELANNE

Photo credits